MW00395310

MERCH LIFE

An Introduction to Using
Merch By Amazon
to Design Shirts and Make Money

Chapters presented as a series of online videos

Chris Green
PBLLC Press, Rehoboth, MA

2015

Merch Life

MERCH LIFE:

An Introduction to Using Merch By Amazon to Design Shirts and Make Money

Green, Christopher John

Hi, Mom!

Copyright © 2015 Chris Green. All rights reserved.

Published by PBLLC Press, Rehoboth, MA 02769

First Printing, October 2015

ISBN-13: 978-1517795993

ISBN-10: 1517795990

Printed in the United States of America

Dedication

This book/course is dedicated to my amazing family. I love you all so much. Jenn, you are the love of my life. Your support in all of my ventures means the world to me. David, you're my awesome panda cub. Abby, you are my sweet, little koala.

Merch Life

About this book:

This book is set up as a video course. Videos that you can view online that will walk you through the Merch by Amazon platform. The videos can be viewed on any computer, tablet, or smartphone. They can be downloaded as well for viewing offline.

As a BONUS for purchasing this book, you get the UDEMY course 100% FREE! Additional downloads for this book/course are available on UDEMY. Updates to this book/course will be posted on UDEMY so be sure to join. Use the code 'book' when signing up at:

https://www.udemy.com/merchbyamazonintro

Or just use this link:

https://www.udemy.com/merchbyamazonintro/?couponCode=book

I also have an ADVANCED UDEMY course that goes into greater depth on shirt ideas and spotting trends from sports, pop culture, news, politics, memes, hashtags, and more. It also covers setting up a branded store, Amazon sales ranks, keyword searches, and much more.

This course normally sells for $197 but use the code 'book' to get it for just $47.

Use code 'book' when signing up at:

https://www.udemy.com/merchbyamazon

Or just use this link:

https://www.udemy.com/merchbyamazon/?couponCode=book

Let's connect! I'd love to hear your ideas and help you succeed with the Merch by Amazon platform. Find me on Facebook at:

http://facebook.com/chris or email me at: chris@chrisgreen.com

I also started a free Facebook Group to discuss the Merch by Amazon platform. Find it at
https://www.facebook.com/groups/merchlife

To your success,

Chris Green

Director, www.merch.life

Merch Life

Table of Contents

NOTES:

Video 1 – Introduction to Merch by Amazon

In this intro video, your instructor, Chris Green, gives an overview of the Merch by Amazon platform.

https://vimeo.com/143097681

To view this video, enter the link on any computer, tablet, or smartphone and enter the PASSWORD: book

NOTES:

Video 2 – Quickstart Video

In this video, we upload the artwork and create a brand new shirt listing on Amazon using Merch by Amazon to show just how easy it is to create product pages. The finer details of this process are broken down in later videos.

https://vimeo.com/143097680

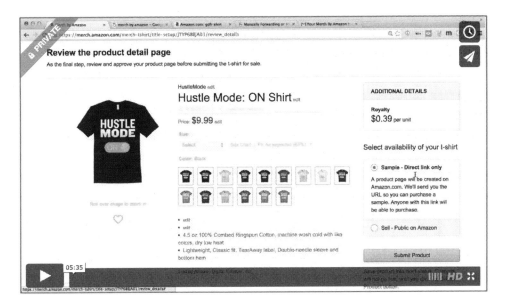

To view this video, enter the link on any computer, tablet, or smartphone and enter the PASSWORD: book

NOTES:

Video 3 – Merch by Amazon – Still Developing

Merch by Amazon is so new that it is developing and changing even as I make the videos for this course! They now have a max price of $49.99 on shirts and are limiting designs to a maximum of five color options. When I made several of the videos in this course, there was no color choice max. So please keep this in mind as you go through the course and open your own Merch by Amazon account that some things may look different over time. I expect many of the changes to be for the better such as more options and more control over the product details. Time will tell.

https://vimeo.com/143097675

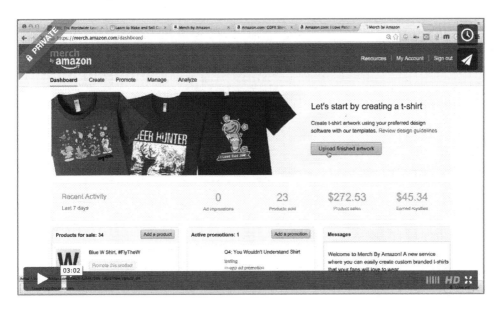

To view this video, enter the link on any computer, tablet, or smartphone and enter the PASSWORD: book

NOTES:

Video 4 – Merch by Amazon – October 2015 Update

Just three weeks into the launch of Merch by Amazon and there are already two big changes!

First, they are limiting the number of shirt designs that a creator can upload. They now have a tiered system where you will be limited on how many listings you can upload related to how many shirts you are actually selling. I was worried that this may happen because in all of my experience with Amazon, I know that they want a great customer experience on the Amazon website and it wouldn't take long for some creators to start uploading 'I Love Frogs' and 'I Love Sushi' and 'I Love Leaves' and then 'Bill Loves Frogs' and 'Bill Loves Sushi' and 'Bill Love Leaves' and then 'Sally Loves Frogs' and well I think you get what I'm trying to say.

BONUS TIP: Even if your shirts aren't selling (yet), you can still up your design limit with a PAY TO PLAY model of just buying your own shirts. Think about it; if your ideas and designs are wrth putting on Amazon, then buying a single copy of one of your shirts should be worth it.

Second, the program has seen such a great response that they are extending their shipping lead times to customers from 2-3 days + Prime shipping to 5-7 days + Prime shipping. This is not something that content creators can control but pass it along to any customers or traffic that you may be sending to your Amazon listings.

https://vimeo.com/143796886

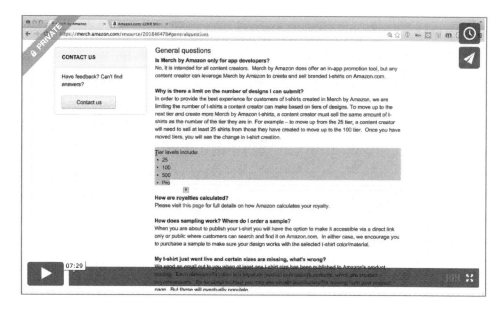

To view this video, enter the link on any computer, tablet, or smartphone and enter the PASSWORD: book

NOTES:

Video 5 – Setting Up Your Account

In this video, we walk through the basic account settings that need to be configured prior to uploading shirt designs. These settings include your business info, your banking info (to receive royalty payments), and your tax information.

https://vimeo.com/143097677

To view this video, enter the link on any computer, tablet, or smartphone and enter the PASSWORD: book

<u>NOTES:</u>

Video 6 – Merch by Amazon - Dashboard

In this video, we take a detailed look at the Merch by Amazon dashboard. The features here include Creating, Promoting, Managing, and Analyzing your items.

https://vimeo.com/143097682

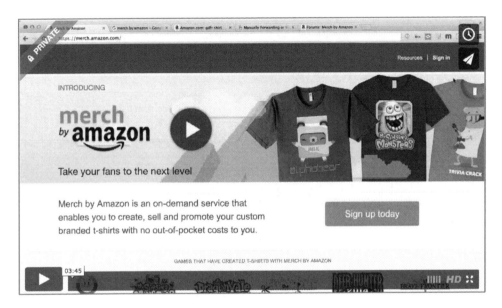

To view this video, enter the link on any computer, tablet, or smartphone and enter the PASSWORD: book

NOTES:

Video 7 – Merch by Amazon Resources

Merch by Amazon provides some amazing resources for their users. In this video, we walk through each section and outline the information in each.

https://vimeo.com/143097683

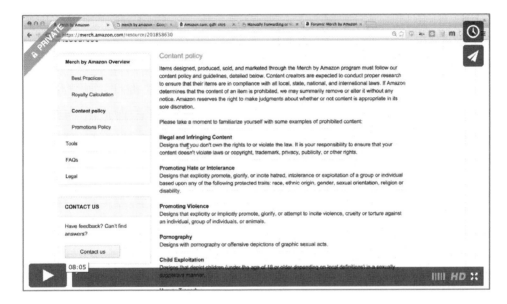

To view this video, enter the link on any computer, tablet, or smartphone and enter the PASSWORD: book

NOTES:

Video 8 – Merch by Amazon TEMPLATE

In this video, we take a detailed look at the Photoshop PSD file and how you can use it to create great Merch by Amazon shirt designs. Direct downloads of Amazon templates included.

https://vimeo.com/143097679

To view this video, enter the link on any computer, tablet, or smartphone and enter the PASSWORD: book

NOTES:

Video 9 – Image Dimensions and Resolution

Merch by Amazon uploads require a PNG file 4500 pixels wide by 5400 pixels high, 300 DPI with a transparent background. Use this to make new shirt designs.

https://vimeo.com/143097674

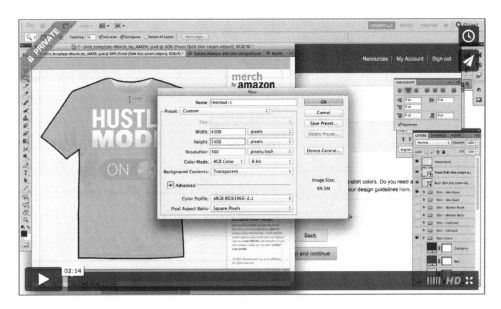

To view this video, enter the link on any computer, tablet, or smartphone and enter the PASSWORD: book

A BLANK Merch by Amazon PSD file with dimensions 4500 x 5400, 300 DPI is available to download in the FREE UDEMY course.

Just use the code 'book' when signing up at:

https://www.udemy.com/merchbyamazonintro

NOTES:

Video 10 - Best Practices - 12" x 12" Image Sizes

I ordered several shirts with the full 4500 x 5400, 300 dpi images used and they are a bit big. This is a 15" x 18" images on a shirt

I will be making many of my shirts with 12" x 12" images moving forward, and this video will show you a few tricks to making sure that they stay centered on the 15" x 18" required template size.

https://vimeo.com/143796686

To view this video, enter the link on any computer, tablet, or smartphone and enter the PASSWORD: book

Amazon's own Best Practices state:

Artwork sizing and placement

While you can certainly use the entire 15" x 18" in space, often customers find a print that is 18 inches to be overwhelming. By and large we find that keeping your maximum dimension to 12 inches or less results in higher conversion rates.

<u>NOTES:</u>

Video 11 – Uploading a Shirt Design, Detail Process

In this video, we do a more detailed walkthrough of the Merch by Amazon upload, design, and product page creation process. We talk about each setting and give examples of when you should use different options.

https://vimeo.com/143097678

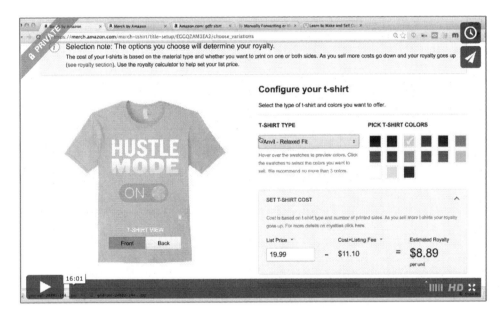

To view this video, enter the link on any computer, tablet, or smartphone and enter the PASSWORD: book

NOTES:

Video 12 – Amazon PRIME and a Powerful Example: GDFR

In this video, see exactly why anyone who uses Merch by Amazon has an unfair advantage when listing on Amazon. We talk about the benefits of being eligible for Amazon Prime and how Merch by Amazon shirts can quickly be the #1 result for searches on Amazon.

https://vimeo.com/143097676

To view this video, enter the link on any computer, tablet, or smartphone and enter the PASSWORD: book

NOTES:

Bonus Photoshop Tutorial #1 - Software

There are a ton of Photoshop CS2 video tutorials on YouTube as well as UDEMY courses on the topic. You may be able to get Photoshop CS2 (older software) for free by following the instructions on this page:

http://www.digitaltrends.com/computing/how-to-get-photoshop-for-free/

Photoshop CC (Creative Cloud) - $9.99/month Photoshop Software

http://www.adobe.com/products/photoshop.html

In most of my videos, I use Photoshop CS5. Full installs of Photoshop can be expensive. Adobe does offer a version for $9.99/month called Photoshop CC (Creative Cloud). In the following videos, I'll show the Photoshop techniques that I use within Photoshop CC. There are many different photo-editing programs out there. Some install on your computer, some run in a browser, some are free and some are paid. There are A TON of free videos online (YouTube especially) with free tutorials for any specific Photoshop task that you are trying to do.

If you use Photoshop CC, PLEASE watch the free tutorial videos in their Welcome section.

https://vimeo.com/143830994

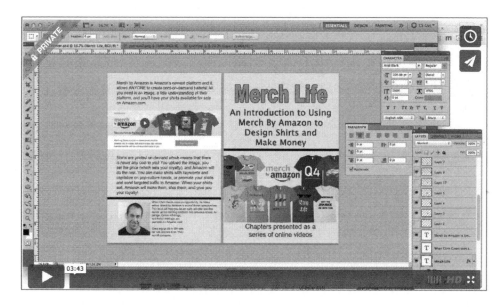

To view this video, enter the link on any computer, tablet, or smartphone and enter the PASSWORD: book

Bonus Photoshop Tutorial #2 – Magic Wand

In this video, we look at using the Photoshop tool called Magic Wand as well as demonstrate Photoshop Layers.

https://vimeo.com/143832753

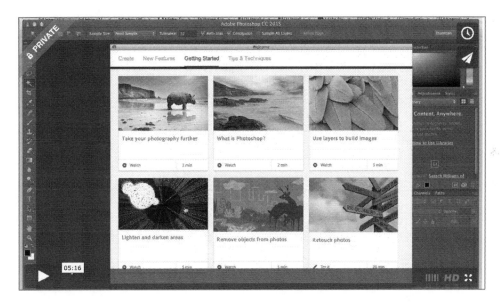

To view this video, enter the link on any computer, tablet, or smartphone and enter the PASSWORD: book

NOTES:

Bonus Photoshop Tutorial #3 - Removing the Background

In this video, we look at a couple of different ways to remove the background from images. Find other ways by searching YouTube. There are also websites and services that will remove the background from your images for you (for a fee).

https://vimeo.com/143833619

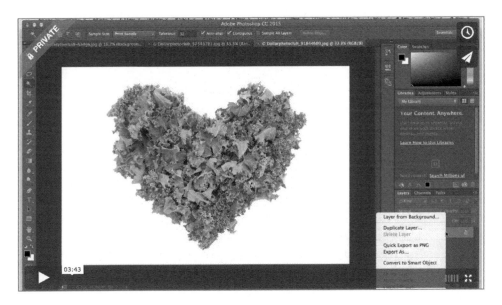

To view this video, enter the link on any computer, tablet, or smartphone and enter the PASSWORD: book

NOTES:

Bonus Photoshop Tutorial #4 – Fonts: Choosing, Resizing, Changing Color, Outlining

In this video, we look at adding and editing TEXT. We look at how to change the font, change the size, stretch and transform, change the color, add outlines, and even arc the text up or down. Adding text to shirts to use with Merch by Amazon is a fast and easy way to get shirts designs up quickly.

https://vimeo.com/143836147

To view this video, enter the link on any computer, tablet, or smartphone and enter the PASSWORD: book

NOTES:

Bonus Photoshop Tutorial #5 - Resizing Images, Cutting, Pasting, Transforming

In this video, we take an image and copy & paste the part that we want to edit into a new image. Then we transform and resize the image. We use the Magic Wand and several keyboard shortcuts. This video will help you learn how to manipulate images in Photoshop.

https://vimeo.com/143836900

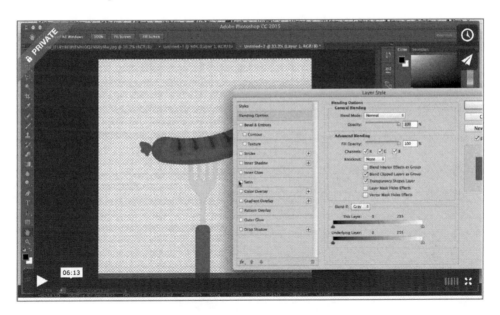

To view this video, enter the link on any computer, tablet, or smartphone and enter the PASSWORD: book

NOTES:

Bonus Photoshop Tutorial #6 - Screen Capture & Cropping

In this video, you'll learn how to take a screen capture or screen cap, create a new image, and paste the screen capture to create an editable image. On Mac, use Command + Control + Shift + 3. For PC, you may have to Google how your setup takes screen captures. Once you have a screen capture created, you can then crop the image to get just the part that you want.

https://vimeo.com/143834687

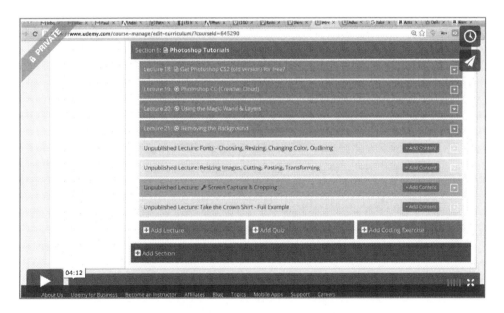

To view this video, enter the link on any computer, tablet, or smartphone and enter the PASSWORD: book

NOTES:

Bonus Photoshop Tutorial #7 - Take the Crown Shirt: Full Example

In this video, see a full example of taking an idea, getting an image, removing the background, copying, pasting, transforming, adding and editing text, and resizing the canvas.

https://vimeo.com/143838395

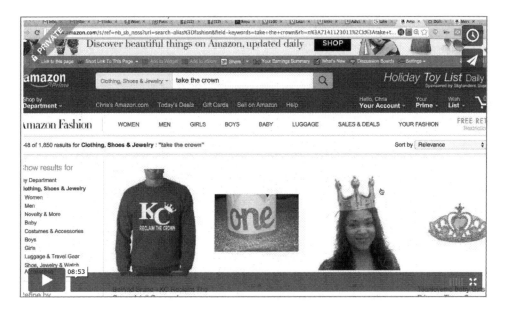

To view this video, enter the link on any computer, tablet, or smartphone and enter the PASSWORD: book

Merch by Amazon – Best Practices

Link to online reference:

https://merch.amazon.com/resource/201849250

How to ensure your t-shirt design will look great

- CYMK: While you may design your t-shirt using RGB color space, your t-shirt will be printed using CYMK. CYMK colorspace is not as wide as RGB; for example, metallics and pastels are difficult to render in CYMK.
- 300 DPI resolution: Your design needs to be 300 DPI, not a lower resolution image resized to 300 DPI. Resizing will result in a pixelated, blocky print.
- Less than 25MB files
- Design the entire t-shirt: You are submitting an 15" x 18" rectangular artwork using our templates; however, you need to consider that your design is being printed on a t-shirt. Your design should integrate into the t-shirt. Generally speaking, you want to avoid a solid rectangle filling the entire printable area. Your design should work with the t-shirt. Where possible consider the (blank) shirt color in your design, by making that color transparent in your artwork.

Artwork sizing and placement

- While you can certainly use the entire 15" x18" in space, often customers find a print that is 18 inches to be overwhelming. By and large we find that keeping your maximum dimension to 12 inches or less results in higher conversion rates.
- Be conscious of the placement of design elements and where they would appear in relation to your customer's anatomy. Remember your designs are printed on men's, women's, and kids shirts.
- Horizontally center designs visually as well as mathematically. Heavy design elements on one side can make a design feel off balance even if it is mathematically centered.

- Designs typically do the best when they are placed near the top of the print area.

Types of designs/effects to avoid

- Designs that look contained within a rectangular block, especially if the design does not incorporate the color of the shirt (taking a screen capture of a game)
- Elements that subtly blend into the shirt color. These can print like a halo with a hard edge. Think how web safe colors have big jumps between colors.
- Elements with a transparency less than 20% are likely to get lost when printing, or turn out as a solid color.
- Designs that have a single, large logo as the only element of the design
- Simple white shirts

Designs that typically sell well

- Designs on dark shirts (our t-shirt color selector is organized based on sales)
- Distressed designs
- Simple, identifiable silhouettes work well with content that has characters
- Bold high contrast colors.
- Larger art elements in the t-shirt design may get better response to online promotions, as subtler designs are hard to see in thumbnail views of the shirt

T-shirt testing

Every brand is different, but what we've found is that most have fans who would love to wear t-shirts with the brand on it. What we never know for sure is what type of designs will appeal to a particular fan base. So we suggest that you test out at least 5 to 6 unique designs. Typically, there are four categories of designs that work well:

1. Logos
2. Funny/ inside jokes
3. Character driven designs, typically doing something
4. Subtle designs that just look "cool" to non-fans, but a true fan will recognize it

We suggest creating at least one design for each category, and then present each design to your fans. See what works and then iterate.

Promotions

How to promote your t-shirts

- Social promotions: you can reach out to your fans, friends, and followers by creating Facebook and Twitter posts directly from Merch by Amazon portal promotions section. You can also pin your t-shirt design on Pinterest from your Amazon product page. You will find your t-shirt's product URL on the dashboard and on the Promote section by selecting your t-shirt.

- Blogs, YouTube, email campaigns, web campaigns: you can reach out to your audience on your blogs, youtube channel, web site promotions, and direct them to your T-shirt product page on Amazon. You will find your T-shirt's product URL on the Dashboard and Promote sections of the Merch portal.

Merch by Amazon – Royalty Calculations

Link to online reference:

https://merch.amazon.com/resource/201858580

How your royalty is calculated

You earn a royalty on every t-shirt sold. Your royalty is based on the list price you set less Amazon's costs and fees. Amazon costs include materials, production and fulfillment. Fulfillment costs include picking and packing your t-shirt when a customer orders it and shipping your t-shirt to the customer—including shipping for Amazon Prime and Free Shipping-eligible orders.

Example

Selling a 1-sided Anvil brand t-shirt on Amazon.com for $19.99.

List price	$19.99
- Amazon listing fee (sale price* 15%)	$3.00
- Amazon costs	$8.10
= Royalty	**$8.89**
Your share of sale price	44.48%

Amazon Listing Fee

Amazon charges a 15% listing fee for t-shirt sales.

Production and Fulfillment costs

Production and fulfillment costs are based on several variables:

1. 1 or 2 sided printing
2. T-shirt material used
3. How many copies of a particular t-shirt design you sell in a week

Base production/fulfillment costs	$8.10
2-sided printing	+$4.00
Using American Apparel t-shirts	+$1.50

Volume discounts

As you sell more copies of a particular t-shirt design during a week (Sunday to Saturday, Pacific time), Amazon's production costs go down. So we pass those savings along to you. A copy is any t-shirt size/color that is printed with a particular design. At the end of the month we'll update your royalties to reflect your discounts.
Discounts are applied only to the week where the sales occurred. Discounts are applied per printed side, so if your shirt has prints on both sides the discount is double.

Copies sold	Per printed side discount
100	-$0.50
200	-$1.00
300	-$1.50
400	-$2.00

Example

For a 2-sided American Apparel t-shirt that sold 400 copies during the week, production/fulfillment cost would be:

Base production/fulfillment cost per copy	$8.10
+ American Apparel cost	+$1.50
+ 2-sided printing	+$4.00
- Volume discount	-$2.00
- 2nd side volume discount	-$2.00
That week's production/fulfillment cost per copy	**$9.60**

Please note, costs and fees are subject to change without notice.

Merch by Amazon – Content Policy

Link to online reference:

https://merch.amazon.com/resource/201858630

Items designed, produced, sold, and marketed through the Merch by Amazon program must follow our content policy and guidelines, detailed below. Content creators are expected to conduct proper research to ensure that their items are in compliance with all local, state, national, and international laws. If Amazon determines that the content of an item is prohibited, we may summarily remove or alter it without any notice. Amazon reserves the right to make judgments about whether or not content is appropriate in its sole discretion.

Please take a moment to familiarize yourself with some examples of prohibited content:

Illegal and Infringing Content
Designs that you don't own the rights to or violate the law. It is your responsibility to ensure that your content doesn't violate laws or copyright, trademark, privacy, publicity, or other rights.

Promoting Hate or Intolerance
Designs that explicitly promote, glorify, or incite hatred, intolerance or exploitation of a group or individual based upon any of the following protected traits: race, ethnic origin, gender, sexual orientation, religion or disability.

Promoting Violence
Designs that explicitly or implicitly promote, glorify, or attempt to incite violence, cruelty or torture against an individual, group of individuals, or animals.

Pornography
Designs with pornography or offensive depictions of graphic sexual acts.

Child Exploitation
Designs that depict children (under the age of 18 or older depending on local definitions) in a sexually suggestive manner.

Human Tragedy
Design that include items that have been collected from the site of a tragedy or are in some way directly connected with a tragedy, excluding certain products which commemorate/memorialize the loss of human life.

Merch by Amazon – Download Shirt Templates

Link to online reference:

https://merch.amazon.com/resource/201851710

Downloadable templates are available for Adobe Illustrator, Adobe Photoshop, and GIMP. Using the Adobe Photoshop (PSD) template Is discussed in Video #8.

Download t-shirt template

We want to print the best possible t-shirt for your brand. For this reason, we have developed a system that allows you to create your t-shirt design in your preferred design software. This allows you to use all the fine-tuning controls you have come to expect when creating a design.

Create your design according to the specifications listed on the t-shirt image to the right. Image specifications: 15"W x 18"H @ 300ppi (i.e. 4500 x 5400 pixels), sRGB, less than 25MB.

Alternatively, download one of our t-shirt templates to use as a guide. These files are preset to the correct design specifications.

- Adobe Illustrator (1.2MB)
- Adobe Photoshop (4.9 MB)
- GIMP (1.4 MB)

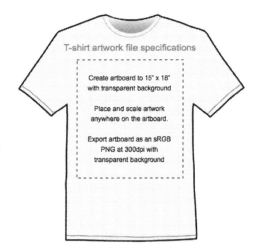

Merch by Amazon – FAQs

Link to online reference:

https://merch.amazon.com/resource/201846470

General questions

Is Merch by Amazon only for app developers?

No, it is intended for all content creators. Merch by Amazon does offer an in-app promotion tool, but any content creator can leverage Merch by Amazon to create and sell branded t-shirts on Amazon.com.

How are royalties calculated?

Please visit https://merch.amazon.com/resource/201858580

for full details on how Amazon calculates your royalty.

How does sampling work? Where do I order a sample?

When you are about to publish your t-shirt you will have the option to make it accessible via a direct link only or public where customers can search and find it on Amazon.com. In either case, we encourage you to purchase a sample to make sure your design works with the selected t-shirt color/material.

My t-shirt just went live and certain sizes are missing, what's wrong?

We send an email out to you when at least one t-shirt size has been published to Amazon's product catalog. Each size/color/fit t-shirt is a separate product in Amazon's systems, which are created asynchronously. So for about an hour you may see certain sizes/colors/fits missing from your product page. But these will eventually populate.

I'd like to purchase a large order of t-shirts for an event, how do I do that?

Currently we do not offer a bulk ordering system. However, you can purchase as many shirts as you'd like directly from Amazon.com. You'll receive a royalty on each sale, and if you order sufficient shirts to get volume discounts, your royalty will be increased.

What t-shirt sizes does Amazon support?

All t-shirts you design will be available in men's, women's, and kid's sizes. Men's sizes range from S-3XL, women's S-XL, and kids k4-k12. All of these sizes will be available from a single Amazon product page, enabling you to easily direct traffic to a single URL.

Can I change the type of t-shirt blank after I publish my design?

Unfortunately, you cannot. However, you can create another product with the same design and use the other t-shirt blank.

I noticed one of my kids Anvil t-shirts was printed on American Apparel, why is this?

At times we may not be able to stock certain kid sizes in Anvil, when this happens we will replace the Anvil kids t-shirt with an American Apparel t-shirt.

Can I change my artwork after I publish my design?

Unfortunately, you cannot.

Can I run a sale on my t-shirt?

Unfortunately, we do not support the ability to show a discounted price on your product page. However, you can always change your t-shirt price through the "Manage" tab.

How is the main product image determined on my t-shirt page?

Initially the first product image customers see on your t-shirt page is randomly chosen by Amazon. However, as soon as customers start to purchase your design, the most popular variation will become the main product image.

What browsers does Merch by Amazon support?

We recommend using the latest versions of Firefox and Chrome.

I want to upload a t-shirt design to Merch by Amazon. Can I submit the same design to another website or t-shirt manufacturer?

Yes. Merch by Amazon is non-exclusive.

Artwork questions

I got an error while trying to upload my artwork, what happened?

Please make sure you are using the supplied Photoshop, Illustrator, and Gimp templates. To ensure that your design prints well, we require designs to match our exact requirements: 15x18in, 300DPI, transparent background, PNG, and no more than 25MB in size.

Do I have to use sRGB color space for my designs?

No. By default we assume your design is sRGB. So if you want to use another colors space (e.g. CYMK), please make sure you embed the color space into your PNG.

How does Amazon print t-shirts?

Amazon uses three different printing techniques to produce your t-shirts: digital, digital screen, and screen printing. For mass production of a t-shirt design (more than 200 t-shirts in a week) we use screen printing, where your image will be color separated into 10 or fewer unique colors and then printed. This process is very similar to the way a magazine is printed, which only uses 4 colors. For one off prints we use digital printers, which print full color

(CYMK) images. For medium scale production (50 to 200 t-shirts) we use a digital screen process, where a base layer of ink is placed down with a screen and then the color portion of the print is done with a digital printer.

How does a 15x18in template work on all shirt sizes?

To ensure that your t-shirt is screen printable, where a single set of screens are used for multiple t-shirt sizes, we have grouped our t-shirt sizes into 3 print sizes. Your image will be auto-resized to each of these three print sizes based on the t-shirt.

Size A: 15x18in (100%)	Size B: 10.8x13in (72%)	Size C: 8.3x9.9in (55%)
Men's 3XL	Men's Small	Kids 6
Men's 2XL	Women's Medium	Kids 4
Men's XL	Women's Small	
Men's Large	Kids 12	
Men's Medium	Kids 10	
Women's XL	Kids 8	
Women's Large		

Shipping questions

What shipping options do my customers get?

Merch by Amazon t-shirts will have the same shipping options available as any other item sold by Amazon. Prime members receive free two-day shipping. If a customer spends more than $35 they receive free Super Saver shipping. All other customers will have the option to purchase ground shipping or pay more for faster shipping.

What countries does Amazon ship to?

Amazon.com ships to more than 75 countries in the world. Please note, international customers will need to pay additional shipping fees.

When will my customers get their t-shirts?

Based on the shipping method a customer chooses, t-shirts are printed and shipped within 3 business days of receiving an order.

Getting paid

I'm an Appstore developer do I have to re-enter my tax and banking information?

We apologize for the inconvenience, but you will need to re-enter all of your information into the Merch by Amazon portal.

I am a U.S. content creator. How do I get paid for my Amazon sales?
We make monthly payments for Amazon sales. For electronic payments, the currency of your payment is determined by your bank's location. Provided your balance due exceeds the payment threshold, we will make payment approximately 30 days after the end of the calendar month in which the sale of a t-shirt occurred. For example, we would make payment for sales of t-shirts that occurred in April at the end of May, which is approximately 30 days after the end of April.

In the U.S., we pay by using electronic funds transfer (EFT), and we make payment when your balance due is more than $0.00.

I am an international content creator. How do I get paid for my Amazon sales?

Content creators with banks in supported countries can receive electronic payments from Amazon. Depending on your bank's location, you may be eligible for either direct deposit or wire payments. At this time we do not support sending checks. From the "My Account" tab in the upper right of this page you can visit the payment and banking section to see if the country your bank is located in is supported at this time.

Prior to Amazon issuing a payment, the payment must meet the applicable threshold based on your payment type:

- Direct Deposit: $0 USD, €0 EUR, £0 GBP, ¥0 JPY, $0 CAD, or $R20 BRL
- Wire: $100 USD, €100 EUR, £100 GBP, ¥10,000 JPY, or $100 CAD

Provided your balance due exceeds the payment threshold, we will remit payment approximately 30 days after the end of the calendar month in which the sale occurred. For example, we would remit payment for sales of t-shirts that occurred in April at the end of May, which is approximately 30 days after the end of April.

My bank is not eligible for electronic payments. Can I still sell on Merch by Amazon?

Unfortunately at this time we do not support paying royalties through checks, so you will need to set up a bank account in a supported country.

Are there any payment thresholds when receiving payments?

Prior to Amazon issuing a payment, the payment must meet the applicable threshold based on your payment type:

- Direct Deposit: $0 USD, €0 EUR, £0 GBP, ¥0 JPY, $0 CAD, or $R20 BRL
- Wire: $100 USD, €100 EUR, £100 GBP, ¥10,000 JPY, or $100 CAD

Where can I see my payments?

You can find your payment information through the "Analyze" tab in the Merch by Amazon portal.

Will you withhold any taxes from payments made to international content creators for sales?

U.S. tax law requires us to report royalty payments made to entities and persons resident outside of the United States, and may require us to withhold and remit taxes on such royalty payments to the Internal Revenue Service (IRS). Although you may also be required to report and pay taxes to your own government, we are not involved in that process. You should consult a tax advisor if you have any questions on these requirements.

Determining Tax Rates

The standard tax-withholding rate applied to royalty payments made to residents outside of the United States is 30%. If you are a non-U.S. developer and your country of residence has an existing income tax treaty with the U.S., provided you furnish us with a valid IRS Form W8-BEN (and/or other required documentation), you may be eligible for a reduced rate of U.S. tax withholding on the royalty payments you receive.

Please note that we will provide both you and the IRS with an IRS Form 1042-S each year, which will provide detail regarding U.S. taxes withheld and remitted to the IRS during that year.

Please refer to the "Tax Interview" section for additional details on how to provide your tax identity information to Amazon.

Promotions questions

How can I get my t-shirt image from the Amazon product page?

Your t-shirt images are available from the Amazon Detail Page, here are the instructions to get high resolution images for your promotions:

1. Go to your product page on Amazon.com
2. Right click – 'page info' (on firefox browser) – 'media tab' on the top. This shows all the images on the page, browse the images and select the high res t-shirt image
3. Open the URL on a browser, change the size to 1500 to get right sized image for the ad creative.

Tax interview questions

What is the tax information interview?

The Tax information interview, located in the Merch by Amazon portal in the **My Account** section under **Tax Information**, is a self-service interview process designed to collect your required taxpayer information to complete an IRS tax form (e.g. IRS Forms W-9 or W-8) which will be used to certify your U.S. or non-U.S. status, determine if your payments are subject to IRS reporting, and the rate of U.S. tax withholding (if any) applicable to your payments..

You can find more information about the tax information interview in the Tax information interview Guide.

I am a U.S. taxpayer. What information do I need to provide to Amazon?

Amazon requires all U.S. content creators, including non-profit and tax-exempt organizations, to provide valid taxpayer identification information by taking the tax information interview in order to comply with U.S. tax reporting regulations before they can start selling t-shirts.

The interview guides you through a step-by-step process gathering all necessary information required to establish your tax identity and generates an IRS Form W-9 for U.S. Payees.

You will be required to provide your U.S. tax identification number (TIN). Your nine-digit federal tax identification number is your Social Security Number (SSN), Employer Identification Number (EIN), or Individual Tax Identification Number (ITIN).

Please retake the interview if your information or circumstances change.

I am an international content creator. I pay taxes in my own country, not the United States. Do I need to provide any information to Amazon?

Yes, Amazon requires all international content creators to provide valid taxpayer identification information by taking the tax information interview in the Merch by Amazon portal. To complete an IRS Form W-8 to certify your non-U.S. status, determine if your payments are subject to U.S. tax reporting, and the rate of U.S. tax withholding (if any) applicable to your payments. A taxpayer identification number (TIN) is not required unless you wish to claim a reduced rate of U.S. withholding tax.

Please retake the interview if your information or circumstances change.

What information will I need to provide in the tax information interview?

You will need to provide U.S. tax status (U.S. person or non-U.S. person), the name of the individual or organization that will report the income on an income tax return, permanent address, and U.S. and/or foreign (non-U.S.) taxpayer identification number (TIN), if applicable.

How do I know if I am a U.S. person?

In general, you are considered a U.S. person if you are a (1) U.S. citizen, (2) U.S. resident, or (3) entity organized under the laws of the U.S.

What name should I provide during the tax information interview?

You should provide the name of the individual or organization that will report the income on an income tax return.

If you are completing the information as an organization, use the name as it appears as follows:

- Trust – The name as it appears on the trust deed
- Partnership – The name as it appears in the partnership agreement
- Corporation – The name as it appears in the certificate of incorporation, or other legal document that formed the corporation

- Other - The name as it appears on the legal document that formed the entity

I am a non-U.S. content creator completing the interview for a company. Does that mean I am an "agent"?

Generally, "agent acting as an intermediary" refers to a business or individual that will receive income on behalf another person. Merely completing the tax interview on behalf of a company does not necessarily make you an agent.

If you are unsure if you are an "agent acting as an intermediary", please contact your tax advisor.

What is a U.S. Tax Identification Number (TIN)?

A U.S. tax identification number (TIN) is issued by the U.S. tax authority (Internal Revenue Service "IRS") and can be a social security number (SSN), individual taxpayer identification number (ITIN), or employer identification number (EIN).

For U.S. persons, this is typically an SSN (generally for individuals) or EIN (generally for companies).

For non-U.S. persons, this is typically an ITIN (individuals) or EIN (generally for non-individual companies). A taxpayer identification number (TIN) is not required for non-U.S. persons unless you wish to claim a reduced rate of U.S. withholding tax. If you are a non-U.S. person and wish to claim a reduced rate of U.S. withholding tax and you do not have a foreign (non-U.S.) TIN issued for income tax purposes by the tax authority in your country of residence, you may apply for a U.S. TIN.

For more information on tax identification numbers, please consult your tax advisor.

I am not a U.S. content creator, and I don't have a U.S. Taxpayer Identification Number. Can I provide my foreign (non-U.S.) tax identification number in the tax information interview?

To claim treaty benefits, you are required to provide a Taxpayer

Identification Number (TIN). If you do not have a U.S. TIN, you may enter the income tax identification number issued by the tax authority in your country of residence. If you do not have a foreign (non-U.S.) TIN issued for income tax purposes by the tax authority in your country, you may apply for a U.S. TIN.

If your income is effectively connected with a U.S. trade or business, you must provide a U.S. TIN.

What happens if I don't provide the required information?

You must provide your taxpayer identification information to become eligible to sell t-shirts through Merch by Amazon.

If you already provided your taxpayer identification information and received notification that the information is invalid, you must retake the tax information interview with valid information within 30 days to avoid your t-shirts being made unavailable for customers to purchase.

I completed the tax information interview. When will I know if the information I have submitted is valid?

In most cases, your tax information will be validated within a few minutes of submission. In rare cases, the validation process can take 7-10 business days. Please note that you will be unable to make changes to your tax information during the validation process.

If we detect that your tax information does not match IRS records, you will be emailed with further instructions for updating your tax information. If you receive notification that the information you supplied is invalid, you will be required to retake the tax information interview with valid information within 30 days to avoid your t-shirts being made unavailable for customers to purchase.

Why might information that I supplied in the tax information interview be invalid?

The information you enter in the tax information interview is compared with IRS database records. We cannot detect why information is determined to be invalid, or advise you on the specific issue with the information you entered. However, here are some things to consider before retaking the tax information interview:

- Misspelling your name, not including your middle initial or middle name, or entering an incorrect Tax Identification Number (TIN) may cause tax information to not match IRS records.
- Use the name and TIN that appear on your Social Security card [SSN], CP565 notice [ITIN], or CP575A notice [EIN], if applicable.
- If you are providing an EIN, use the name that appears on the top line of the address header on your CP575A notice from the IRS if you are providing a business name.

For your security, we will not be able to update your account records if you provide your tax information over the phone or via email. We also cannot disclose to you the tax information you entered in the tax information interview that was invalid.

Check your records to confirm your tax information, and enter this information in the tax information interview.

Will you withhold any taxes from U.S. source payments made to international content creators?

U.S. source payments are subject to a statutory 30% rate of U.S. tax withholding. You may claim a reduced rate of withholding under an income tax treaty by completing an IRS tax form (e.g. Form W-8) in the tax information interview if your country of residence has an income tax treaty with the United States that permits a lower withholding rate for the type of income for which you are receiving payments. To check if your country of residence has an income tax treaty with the United States, please reference the IRS website. Royalty treaty rates can be found in IRS Publication 515. Please note: you must provide a Taxpayer Identification Number (TIN) to claim treaty benefits. If you have a U.S. TIN, you must provide it. If you do not have a U.S. TIN, you may enter the income tax identification number issued by the tax authority in your country of residence. If the tax authority in your country of residence does not issue tax identification numbers for income tax purposes, you may apply for a U.S. TIN.

Please consult your tax advisor if you have questions.

Will I be subject to U.S. tax reporting by the U.S. tax authority (Internal Revenue Service, "IRS")?

U.S. developers that receive royalty payments exceeding the IRS reporting thresholds during the calendar year will receive IRS Form 1099-MISC on or before January 31 of the year following payment. For example, calendar year 2015 payments will be reported on or before January 31, 2016. This form will also be reported to the U.S. tax authority (Internal Revenue Service "IRS").

Non-U.S. providers that receive U.S. source royalty payments during the calendar year will receive IRS Form 1042-S on or before March 15 of the year following payment detailing payments received and any associated U.S. tax withholding. For example, calendar year 2015 payments will be reported on or before March 15, 2016. This form will also be reported to the U.S. tax authority (Internal Revenue Service "IRS").

Made in the USA
Middletown, DE
23 July 2020

13424396R00042